Archbishop Romero
Ten Years On

Julian Filochowski

Archbishop Oscar Romero
Tenth Anniversary Lecture

 Catholic Institute for International Relations
Catholic Fund for Overseas Development

First published March 1991

Catholic Institute for International Relations (CIIR)
22 Coleman Fields, London N1 7AF, England

Catholic Fund for Overseas Development (CAFOD)
2 Romero Close, Stockwell Road, London SW9 9TY, England

© Julian Filochowski 1991

This text is an edited version of a lecture given at Heythrop College, London, on 13 November 1990.

ISBN 1 85287 082 6

Cover design by Rich Cowley

Printed in England by the Russell Press Ltd
Radford Mill, Norton Street, Nottingham NG7 3HN

El Salvador today is racked by civil war, accompanied by merciless torture and killings, and colossal human suffering — much the same as it was a year ago — and ten years ago. In this tiny nation of Central America, named in honour of Christ the Saviour, they have lived out over the last 20 years, in an extraordinary way, the agonies and struggles of our divided world and the pains and tensions of a disunited church.

On 24 March 1990 there was an outpouring of joy in San Salvador as the tenth anniversary of the assassination and martyrdom of Archbishop Oscar Arnulfo Romero was marked in great style. There were echoing celebrations throughout Latin America, across Europe and North America and indeed all over the world. The killing of Archbishop Romero, or the 'magnicide', as they now call it in Spanish, took place when a marksman's bullet hit its target and entered his body as he celebrated a memorial Requiem Mass that Monday evening in 1980. One year ago this week, in the midst of a new offensive in El Salvador's civil war, the wheel came full circle and in another explosion of hatred against the church emanating from the military radio and military high command, six Jesuit priests at the Catholic University — the UCA — and their two domestic helpers, Julia Elba and Celina, were slaughtered. Tonight, 13 November, is the anniversary of the military search of their community home; personally authorised, it is now known, by President Cristiani himself, it was the crucial preliminary sweep for the murderous operation of 16 November.

The lives, the work and the deaths of the Jesuits were intimately entwined with Archbishop Romero's, and we have lived once again the mourning and the martyrdom: the death of great, good and gifted individuals and the resurrection seen in the people of El Salvador, in the university and in the Society of Jesus.

Beginnings
Monseñor, as Archbishop Romero is affectionately called by the ordinary people of El Salvador, was a great gift of God to his country. As a bishop

and martyr he is a precious gift to the universal church. I want to suggest that in Archbishop Romero we have an archetypal exponent of the vital church of Medellín and Puebla, an episcopal role model for Latin America, an extraordinary paradigm of the preferential option for the poor and a patron saint for the whole justice and peace enterprise of the post-Vatican II church.

I came to know Central America, the Jesuits there, and Archbishop Romero through CIIR and in particular its Overseas Programme, with which I served for three-and-a-half years in Central America. The great integrity of CIIR was to follow through the experience of their overseas workers in that area with lobbying and advocacy in international fora in pursuit of human rights and social justice in this troubled region — and at a time when it was neither fashionable nor popular to do so. The solidarity with people and church in Central America which CIIR has generated and steadfastly shown over 25 years has been remarkable and very greatly appreciated.

I remember Romero's appointment as Archbishop of San Salvador early in 1977. The backdrop was appalling rural poverty and an absolute refusal on the part of the wealthy to countenance land reform; electoral fraud, military dominated government and human rights violations; an incipient rural peasant movement and a church sympathetic to, increasingly present with, and accompanying the poor.

But Romero was the choice for Archbishop of General Molina, the then military President, he was the choice of the coffee barons, and certainly not the Jesuits' preferred candidate, nor indeed CIIR's; they had hoped that the then auxiliary bishop Rivera Damas would get the job. The landed elite expected Romero to douse what they saw as the dangerous social activism among the clergy and to keep the church well away from controversial political and economic issues. Happily, he grievously failed them.

I will not chart for you in detail the path he trod over three years to his Calvary. It is patently clear that he was a man who continually grew in his personal spiritual life and grew into his role of church leader. Crises which might have blocked or intimidated a lesser man became opportunities for grace and conversion, for growth and redoubled commitment. The killing, within weeks of his installation, of Jesuit Father Rutilio Grande, an intimate personal friend, was one key moment which pulled the scales from his eyes. It led him to testify, before the whole country and the world beyond, to the appalling situation in the Salvadorean countryside by speaking out the truth, clearly, unambiguously, indeed prophetically.

But his archiepiscopal ministry became imbued with that same terrible truth and his own actions as Archbishop and the work of the many organisations of the archdiocese were utterly consistent and at one with the prophetic message he spoke. While on the one hand he set up a practical service to protect human rights and document their abuse, he also adamantly refused to allow himself to be instrumentalised to bless the social and economic status quo. He increasingly realised that here were structures of sin which brought death to his people.

He came to be known, and was one of the first to be known, as the 'voice of the voiceless'. He was the pastor who anchored his message, his questions and his denunciations in gospel values. He was the teacher who 'did theology' with his people from the pulpit to show them that their lives and their daily concerns were a fundamental part of God's plan. As he walked with the poor and encouraged them to organise to secure their rights he always eschewed violence. Without any naivety about the violence of the state, he continually urged and sought a peaceful route to political and social change. He intervened to find the whereabouts and secure the release not only of tortured and disappeared prisoners but also of the kidnapped businessmen and diplomats taken by the guerrilla groups.

Prophet, priest, teacher, communicator, peacemaker, theologian, advocate and martyr, he was utterly orthodox in all. His diary is the proof if proof be needed. Unedited and unexpurgated, it was published to coincide with the tenth anniversary of his death. Bishop Pedro Casaldáliga of Brazil said the publication of this intimate testament was the most glorious celebration of the subversive memory of *Monseñor*, alive in his people. The diary is in fact the transcript of daily cassette recordings he made.

To listen to the tapes and to read the diary brought reminders to me of John XXIII's *Journal of a Soul*. The prophet Romero to the end of his life is a man rooted in tradition, with many fine conservative traits. The simplicity of the man which was so evident in his way of life is palpable. The humility which hits you from the pages is authentic. His religiosity and prayer life are clearly crucial to his daily existence. And it is the spirituality which gives him strength. One of the mental snapshots of the man that I retain after three visits to him in San Salvador is of when he shyly asked me whether I knew of other dioceses in Latin America coping with conflicts and persecutions or whether San Salvador was an absolutely isolated case. He knew few bishops beyond Central America and had only the faintest idea of the troubles of the church in Brazil, Chile and other places. I remember seeing relief break out on his face as I spoke to him of the trials and tribulations of Cardinal Arns and Dom Adriano Hipólito from Brazil, Carlos Camus in Chile, Bishop Proaño in Ecuador, and others. I recall too how after a good number of days with him at Puebla he pleaded with me for help in dealing with the cohorts of the international press. All those memories are dramatically enhanced for me by the diary. It portrays the days of dilemmas and doubts, of a man always so loyal to the Magisterium, so overjoyed at his affirmation by Paul VI, so hurt by those fellow bishops in El Salvador who remained blind to his intentions and by the many insensitivities of the Curia in Rome whose sight and hearing, where El Salvador was concerned, seemed to be perpetually defective. He articulates so frequently his concern to reinforce and underpin the real unity of the archdiocese and particularly the oneness of its family of priests.

There is no political ideologue, no hidden agenda, no dupe and no fellow traveller. Only a man who tries to see the best in those he meets, who tries to highlight the positive in every encounter and to impute reasonable and rational motives as far as possible to everyone.

We have in Oscar Romero the 'evangeliser' par excellence who preached the gospel of Jesus Christ in season and out of season and he sought by every means within his power to transform that Good News of the gospel into a reality for the poor and the marginalised. He laboured to incarnate the church and the archdiocesan structures in the crude realities of El Salvador and the lives of its people. Not by selling out to a political creed or faction. Not by turning his back on the liturgy or abandoning ecclesial symbols, or by tearing up tradition or scorning orthodoxy.

On the contrary, he demonstrated that orthodox Catholic Christianity, in order to be faithful to Vatican II's Constitution on the Church in the Modern World, to Paul VI's *Evangelii Nuntiandi*, to the Medellín and Puebla commitments, demanded this wholehearted insertion and immersion in the world.

It involved choices and taking sides in the midst of conflict, injustice and sin. It involved the valuing of every human person, their rights and dignity, no matter their origin, class or ideology. Rich and poor alike were offered redemption and salvation. Yet there was a preferential option for the deprived and impoverished, the widow and orphan, which had to go way beyond mere slogans and even beyond ecclesiastical documents and preaching.

But he did preach, and regularly, and at length. And he inspired with his preaching. He teased out the powerful lessons of the biblical texts by interpreting them afresh in the context of people's lives in El Salvador. The famous weekly homilies, all of which are now published, are full of beautiful insights and analysis and quotable quotes. They show always a pastor speaking with great freshness, simplicity and eloquence but never ever the demagogue or rabble-rouser his enemies suggested. And towards the end not a few people and groups had identified Romero as their enemy!

The space, the tranquillity and the peace at the very core of his being was his absolute and unconditional trust in God which he nurtured and patiently developed in the hidden dimension of his life — his life of prayer. In the midst of the most searing trials he could turn inwards to draw on that spring for strength and courage.

The atmosphere in El Salvador in the weeks leading up to his death was electric. There was a visceral hatred in the air for the church's commitment to social and political change and for Romero in particular. He had received more than one serious death threat and it is clear that he knew he was going to die.

The notes of his spiritual exercises four weeks before his death show him wrestling with his fear. In the week before his death he scolded his vicars general for not yet having carried out his wishes to appoint new canons to the cathedral chapter, and he ordered them do so immediately. The quorate chapter would be necessary to appoint a vicar capitular to run the diocese if he was killed.

It seems likely that his homily on 23 March triggered the assassination plan. In it he implored soldiers in the security forces to halt the killings with the words 'I beg you, I order you, in the name of God stop the repression.' On the afternoon of the 'magnicide' he broke all his established routines to make time to go to confession. He told his confessor 'he wanted to be clean when he met God'. He was shot with the sniper's bullet at 6.30pm on 24 March and died almost immediately from massive haemorrhaging.

According to testimony in 1987 from one Antonio Amado Garay, who confessed to having driven the assassin's getaway car, the killing was meticulously planned and organised by Captain Rafael Saravia, it was financed through the notorious former Major Roberto D'Aubisson, and carried out, that is the trigger pulled, by Antonio Regalado, a dentist and death squad organiser from Santiago de Maria who became D'Aubisson's head of security when the latter was president of Congress. One attempt to have Saravia extradited from the US was thwarted in 1988 by the Salvadorean Supreme Court. Accusations against D'Aubisson have been aired at election times in El Salvador but D'Aubisson's ARENA party's control of Congress ensured that nothing ever came of it. For the rest, ten years on, nobody has been charged, let alone put on trial, for the murder of the Metropolitan Archbishop of San Salvador, assassinated as he said mass.

The tradition of Oscar Romero

The Salvadorean legal and political system may have allowed his killers to be forgotten. But of course Oscar Romero, bishop and martyr, is remembered. He is present, just as he predicted, in the hearts of the Salvadorean people. His martyrdom is evoked in the struggles of the poor to secure their rights and their freedoms right across the continent. In Latin America the roll call of 20th-century martyrs is already a very long one. It contains hundreds of names of lay people, priests, and religious. But there are hundreds more whose names and deaths have not been documented. They were committed Christians, simple women and men, catechists, delegates of the Word, and courageous members of basic ecclesial communities who freely gave their lives for their friends in the pursuit of a just life. Or — put differently — in their particular historical contexts they 'patiently accepted death for the cause of their faith' (which I understand is the classical definition of true martyrdom). At the head of this only partly visible martyrology is the renowned and venerated name of Oscar Romero who in a real way represents them all.

In life Romero was acclaimed as the 'voice of the voiceless' in El Salvador. Jon Sobrino suggests aptly that in death he has become the 'named of the nameless', being the personification and visible identification of so many human lives taken away needlessly, cruelly, often unremarked and unrecognised. The death toll in El Salvador's conflict and civil war stands at between 70,000 and 75,000 — and rises every week.

I am fond of saying that *Monseñor* was like a comet passing through the heavens the like of which is only seen once in a generation. Others have drawn parallels between his three years at the head of the archdiocese and the public ministry of Jesus. The murdered Jesuit Ignacio Ellacuría used to say, 'With Archbishop Romero, God passed through El Salvador.' Many people don't like these kinds of words, but many others are convinced of it. And if it is true, if God did pass through this world with *Monseñor*, it's not surprising, indeed it is to be expected, that he should have left a lasting imprint among us. That imprint or footprint of God in our world is what is being called today the tradition of Archbishop Romero.

That tradition has developed and flowered around his person year by year. The local celebration of the tenth anniversary culminated in a mass at his cathedral tomb with 16 bishops from three continents, 100 priests, and thousands of people inside the cathedral, and thousands more outside. The 'places' of *Monseñor* have become 'holy places', the chapel where he fell, the little rooms which were his home at the hospital, and of course his tomb, which has become a place of pilgrimage like that of St Thomas à Becket of Canterbury and St Stanislaus of Krakow, archiepiscopal martyrs before him. His day has also been made sacred. 24 March now has its own special Romero identity for which there are great and long preparations all over El Salvador and indeed far beyond. In some places in the diocese they use that day to begin to tell the young children about *Monseñor* and what he did. His name is revered in a whole generation of young Oscar Arnulfos growing up, with almost every Salvadorean village and refugee settlement having its quota. There are Romero centres, Romero libraries, even a street named 'Romero Close' in London! He has inspired books, poems, songs, plays, hymns, films, posters, postage stamps, even an operetta. He is already credited with several miracles and the granting of very many extraordinary favours. There is a great deal of veneration and popular devotion round his person — in short there is no doubt the people have in their own terms canonised him.

The beatification process

These are some of the external signs that Archbishop Romero has in some true sense been 'recognised and sanctified'. His beatification was first proposed in 1980 and CIIR played a part in ensuring that an initial petition reached Rome. It began with the words

> In keeping with the age-old tradition of the church we wish to petition for the proclamation of the sanctity of Mgr Romero, so that he may be presented as a model of a Christian, of a priest, and of a bishop, and so that the faithful may find in him a powerful intercessor before God.

It discussed his martyrdom, his personal virtues, his episcopal ministry and concluded:

> We judge it very right and proper that the church should officially recognise the sanctity of Mgr Romero. Such an act would be to the glory of God, for the pride of the church, and an inspiration and hope for the faithful.

Unfortunately the petition did not prosper at the time. It is not surprising. With the exception of his friend and confidant Bishop Rivera, Romero was cordially disliked and dismissed by the rest of El Salvador's bishops' conference. His relationships with these other four bishops were turbulent. None of the four, including Bishop Revelo, his own auxiliary at the time, attended his funeral. Bishop Aparicio of San Vicente, in an amazing declaration to journalists, of whom I was one, at Puebla in 1979, said that Romero was an egotistical, vain man looking for international fame and notoriety and also manipulated by the Jesuits, who, he said incidentally, were responsible for planting bombs at military barracks!

It was not only the far right of the political spectrum which held to the far-fetched theory that the FMLN guerrillas had murdered Romero. The four bishops and others in the church, inside and outside El Salvador, were very ready to accept this explanation. Bishop Rivera Damas was for three years Apostolic Administrator, or a sort of 'locum', in San Salvador without definitive appointment as Romero's successor until 1983 — which was a reflection of the continuing tension and antipathy towards Romero's pastoral programmes with which Rivera was broadly identified in the bishops' conference.

During the papal visit in 1983 the Holy Father went and prayed at Romero's tomb but he chose his words very carefully and the word 'martyr' was never employed to describe Romero in his speeches at that time. Nevertheless John Paul II became increasingly interested in this controversial figure of Romero and it is rumoured that he secured Polish translations of Romero's sermons and subsequently became convinced of Romero's integrity and orthodoxy. It may be that the murder of the Jesuits a year ago finally clinched the matter. That such an equally abominable crime could be committed ten years on, after so much breast-beating and rationalistion, and so many promises of reform, was a backdated affirmation of how intrinsically related were an *odium iustitiae* and an *odium fidei* in Romero's death.

There followed, around the end of 1989 and the beginning of 1990, a plethora of semi-official affirmations of the martyrdom in El Salvador, most notably from curial Cardinal Silvestrini on the 12 January in Rome. These were surely a prelude to the announcement in San Salvador in March that Father Rafael Urrutia had been officially named postulator for the cause of Archbishop Romero's beatification. The week-long tenth anniversary celebrations were a tremendous launching-pad for the beatification process and Archbishop Rivera's homily on 24 March was one of the strongest eulogies he had ever made of his close friend, Oscar Romero.

These are all the external signs of the 'tradition of Romero'. But Jon Sobrino is surely right to say that we truly remember our martyrs insofar as we carry on the work they have started and follow the insights they have revealed to us. 'Do this in memory of me' should be our guide.

The Romero tradition lives on in the work he inspired, and the continuation of the work he began. Most particularly in the Archdiocese of San Salvador, which has kept flying the banner of a church accompanying the poor, a church alongside, sustaining and protecting the victims of repression, a church offering itself as a servant in the pursuit of reconciliation and peace in the never-ending war, a church which doggedly denounces week by week the atrocities and violations of human rights. Archbishop Rivera has continued Archbishop Romero's ministry and has made an extraordinary personal contribution in attempts to bring together the warring factions and mediate in the peace process. Yet he himself has had to endure a continuing barrage of criticism from many of the other bishops. He has been threatened and denounced by the far right and has too often and quite unjustly been contrasted negatively with his martyred predecessor. Rivera is a great man in the mould of his Salesian brother Cardinal Raúl Silva Henríquez of Chile. I believe Rivera too ought to be named a cardinal of the church.

With him is his vicar general, Mgr Ricardo Urioste, who more than any other prelate has interpreted Archbishop Romero and faithfully followed his path in preaching, teaching, in valiant work with the refugees and displaced, and in helping steer the archdiocese and prevent it from being blown off course. There is also María Julia Hernández, who heads Tutela Legal, the legal aid office of the archdiocese. She has made possible the continuing prestigious human rights work of the church in San Salvador. And finally the auxiliary bishop, Gregorio Rosa Chávez, who has also been of key importance alongside Rivera in keeping the tradition of Romero alive.

More generally around the world the tradition and memory of Archbishop Romero are kept alive by myriads of groups and individuals who inspired by him have demonstrated an enduring solidarity and support for the people of El Salvador.

The Jesuits of the UCA

But there is one other group and institution in El Salvador which to my mind has directly and authentically kept the memory of *Monseñor* alive and kept going the work he began — and that is the Jesuits of the UCA, the Central American University, in San Salvador. We naturally think particularly of those who gave their lives a year ago.

Ignacio Ellacuría, the rector, was philosopher, theologian and political scientist. He steered the university into playing a key role in the continuing search for peace. He was the inspiration and brains behind the national debate for peace, a forum which brought together the whole spectrum of social groups in a major quest for peace. 'Ellacu', as we knew him, became a unique spokesman for dialogue and reconciliation. It is ironic that just before his death he had been involved in discussions with the FMLN guerrillas, trying in vain to dissuade them from the planned new offensive in San Salvador. He was most likely the principal target of the military swoop. Segundo Montes ran the University's Institute of Human Rights and played a particular role in securing the safe return of many refugee communities who had been for years in exile in Honduras and who feared, with good reason, the reaction of the army and government to their return.

Juan Ramón Moreno and Amando López worked in theological reflection and teaching, particularly with the base communities. Ignacio Martin-Baró, teacher and social psychologist, was also involved in surveying public opinion and public attitudes which became the basis for fundamental research and analysis on the crucial economic and social issues facing the country. Joaquín López y López, nicknamed 'Lolo', promoted community development projects, small training programmes, technical workshops and all kinds of different micro-projects which enabled shanty-town communities to help themselves under the umbrella of the organisation Fe y Alegría. But more than individually — as a community with their colleagues who have survived, Jon Sobrino, Jon Cortina, Rodolfo Cardenal, Rogelio Pedraz, and others — they transformed the UCA into a dynamic centre of thought and action within Salvadorean society. With all its offshoots, its galaxy of publications and its creative initiatives, it was an uncomfortable loudspeaker which told the truth about what was going on, which audaciously questioned the very structures of Salvadorean society, which proposed new alternatives obeying the logic of the majorities and not the logic of the elites, and trained people to serve their society and their country however they chose to do so. The voice of the UCA, the voice of the Jesuits, challenged and angered the army, the government, and the wealthy classes, and despite the bitter reactions and many threats, they faithfully carried on the task — regularly invoking the example of Archbishop Romero.

A year ago this week I remember sitting in a conference centre in London reading the fax that had just come through from San Salvador with a transcript of some of the broadcasts on the army radio station virulently attacking the church, and particularly the Jesuits — but I was most struck by the arrogant and venomous tone of the remarks addressed to Archbishop Rivera and Bishop Rosa Chávez, advising them to go to Cuba where they might feel more at home, and I became very frightened. I feared that the unthinkable might actually happen again — in a carbon copy killing of Rivera.

I knew Rivera had been persuaded to travel with a good deal more security for his person than Archbishop Romero had ever had — but if they decided to kill him in anger and fury at the church, nothing would protect him in the end. We suggested to our bishops' conference that a letter of support be sent to Archbishop Rivera. It was agreed it would be despatched on the Friday and publicised at the bishops' press conference. Well, we were wrong and we were too late. The anger erupted but its victims were to be the constantly vilified Jesuits of the UCA. When a military squad searched the community residence on 13 November and found nothing, the Jesuits had then felt secure that nothing terrible would befall them. The search, it turned out, was an intelligence gathering operation to identify exactly who resided where in the house. On the night of the 16th a uniformed patrol of the elite US-trained Atlacatl batallion entered the residence and shot dead all six Jesuits inside and also their two domestic workers, Julia Elba and Celina. They were sleeping in a spare room inside the residence because they were frightened to sleep in their normal quarters at the gatehouse. Obdulio, Julia Elba's husband, who had remained there, was the one who discovered the bodies next morning. He planted a rose garden where their bodies were found.

The explosion of international indignation seemed to surprise the government and the military. The latter's hatred perhaps blinded them to the potential consequences of their butchery. Of the six murdered Jesuits four at least were well-known, regular and distinguished visitors around the world, notably in Spain and the United States, but far beyond too. They were known to the press, to universities, throughout the Society of Jesus, to Conferences of Religious, to aid agencies and human rights bodies, and even in foreign ministries to whose officials they had frequently given important briefings on the national situation.

Archbishop Rivera said the next day, as it became clear from eye-witness accounts precisely what had happened, 'It is the same people who killed Archbishop Romero who have killed the Jesuits.' He might have added, 'and for the same reasons'. Once again the Salvadorean government produced a cock-and-bull story about leftist guerrillas carrying out the atrocities, and sent delegations across the world to propagate their lie: they even persuaded the president and secretary of the bishops' conference to echo the story. This duo managed to secure an audience with Pope John Paul II to try to explain to him that the Jesuits had been killed by FMLN terrorists. Unhappily for them, on the day in mid-January when they arrived back in San Salvador, President Cristiani, under threat of a cut-off of military aid by the US Congress, announced that in fact the killings had been carried out by eight members of his security forces including a colonel, a lieutenant and two sub-lieutenants.

Since then there has been minimal progress. It is inconceivable that Colonel Benavides, the army commander for the area where the university is located, should alone have taken the decision to have the Jesuits murdered. Key documents from the barracks have been burned and others have disappeared. The welter of military witnesses who were finally smoked out to give evidence to investigating Judge Zamora, when military aid again seemed in jeopardy in the US Senate, have carefully and comprehensively contradicted one another. The Salvadorean Jesuit provincial has already documented over 300 inconsistencies. The only evidence against Colonel Benavides is from his co-accused and such evidence in El Salvador is inadmissible for conviction if the case ever comes to court. No army officer has ever been found guilty of a political killing in El Salvador. We are now, I fear, en route to the possible conviction of a handful of young and junior soldiers who carried out the massacre obeying orders from above — after which the case will be regarded as closed.

After the four US churchwomen were raped and killed in December 1980, four lowly soldiers were eventually convicted and imprisoned and the case is regarded as solved — when we know it is unimaginable that such an act against four religious, US citizens, would or could have been taken without a decision from the senior ranks of the security forces.

All this legal process comes at the end of a $9.2 million US aid programme, all to improve the operations and efficiency of El Salvador's courts. It comes, more importantly, at the end of a decade which saw $5 billion of US aid to El Salvador of which $1 billion was purely military aid to equip, train and supposedly professionalise the Atlacatl battalion and other similar units of the security forces. It is the prospect of this aid being cut off which has brought what meagre results have been achieved so far. For the time being at least, the US Congress has cut off 50% of military aid to El Salvador for 1991, reducing it from $85 million to $42.5 million after Democrat Congressman Joe Moakley from Boston, who has headed a US Congress Task Force looking into the killings, declared on 15 August 1990,

> I believe that the High Command of the Salvadorean military is engaged in a conspiracy to obstruct justice in the Jesuits' case. Salvadorean military officers have withheld evidence, destroyed evidence, falsified evidence and repeatedly perjured themselves in testimony before the judge. I do not believe this could have been done without the tacit consent of the High Command. Even more importantly, I believe that the High Command's goal, from the beginning, has

been to control the investigation and to limit the number and rank of the officers who will be held responsible for crimes. As a result some individuals who may have direct knowledge of the murders have been shielded from serious investigation.

No such pressures as these were ever placed to secure the trial and conviction of Archbishop Romero's killers, but so far that is the only significant difference in the untangling of the two crimes. Meanwhile the less famous continue to disappear and die at the hands of the death squads, to suffer torture and extrajudicial execution in connection with military raids, and imprisonment which violates all basic norms. This is the damning verdict of an Amnesty International report as recently as 24 October 1990.

But this week in San Salvador and around the world we are celebrating — celebrating the death and resurrection of these Jesuit martyrs. Their blood too has been the seed of new hope. In the Society of Jesus, in the whole UCA, there is new, resumed life and high morale. Six Jesuits died: a hundred offers came from around the world to take their places. There are record numbers of students seeking to sign on for matriculation and study at the UCA. There has been an outpouring of solidarity in the form of posthumous doctorates, prizes, medals and publications from colleges, from universities and from all kinds of unlikely institutions across the globe which have for the first time felt touched and outraged by the sufferings of the Salvadorean people.

Besides the university itself and its Romero Chapel, the focal points of many ceremonies, liturgies and demonstrations this week will be the two new towns in El Salvador founded by returning refugees. They have been named with great pride and great ceremony. 'Ciudad Segundo Montes' is in the province of Morazán and 'Ciudad Ignacio Ellacuría' is in Chalatenango.

The Jesuits are being remembered; they will continue to be remembered. The work they did, which was the work which Romero did, will go on.

El Salvador's gift to the universal church

For these last 25 years Latin America has been the scene of great suffering, oppression, and cruel military dictatorship. The hopes and aspirations of the poor, the lights that have been ignited, the torches they have carried, have been brutally snuffed out. The ferment in society has been accompanied by a ferment in the church. In struggling to come to terms and to relocate its mission, the Latin American church has been able to offer to the universal church great creativity, challenging theological insights, powerful examples of prophetic witness and a new way of 'being church' among the poor.

In a real sense El Salvador has been at the epicentre. There, intransigent greed and materialism are pitted against the rightful demands of the poor.

Yet this prototypical north-south struggle has been overlaid with an east-west gloss and interpretation to justify massive foreign military aid, civil war, torture, imprisonment, disappearance and summary execution.

And there, too, is a church which has wholeheartedly embraced its mission to announce a civilisation of love and justice, a commitment to bring life, protect life, and secure life to a people surrounded by death and the idols of death.

Romero, the Jesuits, and the Salvadorean church have given us a liberation theology, lived in the furnace of daily struggle, not something ponderously set out in text books. They have given us base communities as living, thriving cells of the Body of Christ, an option for the poor as a beacon for its mission and a commitment to speaking the truth as its regular discourse. And they have given us a gallery of martyrs who have hungered and thirsted for the sake of justice. In Oscar Romero the whole church has been given a great saint, a saint for our times, who kept orthodoxy and orthopraxis in harmony, and found that fine integration between the immanent and the transcendent, the church in the world today. In 1992 Latin America, in celebrating the 500 years since the arrival of Christopher Columbus, will no doubt commemorate some of the great moments of the church's evangelising mission in Latin America. Perhaps too it will look back on some of the less great moments with an appropriate *mea culpa*. My fervent hope is that Pope John Paul II will seize this wonderful opportunity at the Fourth General Conference of Latin American bishops, to be held in Santo Domingo towards the end of 1992, to announce the beatification of Archbishop Romero. 'Such an act would be to the glory of God, for the pride of the church, and an inspiration and hope for the faithful.'

Saint Oscar Romero of San Salvador pray for us.

Related titles published by CIIR

A Decade of War: El Salvador Confronts the Future
Anjali Sundaram and George Gelber (eds)

A review of the history of the conflict in El Salvador and an analysis of the political and social forces as both sides face a new era.

ISBN 1 85287 045 1   269pp   £8.99.

El Salvador: A Spring Whose Waters Never Run Dry

A unique collection of moving testimonies from Christians in refugee camps, shanty towns, base communities and war zones which gives new depth to the meaning of solidarity and Christian faith.

ISBN 1 85287 079 6   96pp   £4.99

Romero: Martyr for Liberation

Archbishop Romero's sermon on the church and liberation, his last homily, and an essay by Jon Sobrino SJ analysing his evangelical ministry and his defence of the oppressed.

ISBN 0 946848 49 1   76pp   £2.95.

In Memoriam: The Jesuit Martyrs of El Salvador

Includes a comprehensive narrative of the background to the events of 16 November 1989, biographies of those murdered, and some of their own writings.

ISBN 1 85287 076 1   180pp   £6.50.

All available from CIIR, 22 Coleman Fields, London N1 7AF.

New address from 1 July 1991: Unit 3, Canonbury Yard, 202-208 New North Road, London N1 7BJ.